TO: _____

FROM: _____

Where Joy Begins
A Little Book of Hope

Where Joy Begins
A Little Book of Hope

Chris Shea

**Andrews McMeel
Publishing**

Kansas City

ISBN: 0-7407-2771-0

Library of Congress Control Number: 2002103775

In Memory of
Doug Kratz

Dear Weary World,

What do we do
when our hearts
are breaking

and most of
our joy
is gone?

What could we
get for
each
other

that might
bring back
some sense
of
hope?

A cottage by
a pond on a big
piece of
land
might provide us
the space
our hearts need
to heal.

Or maybe a
telescope
that only
finds
blue sky

when above us
we see only
black.

A nice woolen sweater
could warm us
when the
world seems so
suddenly
cold.

Dear Weary World,

What do we do

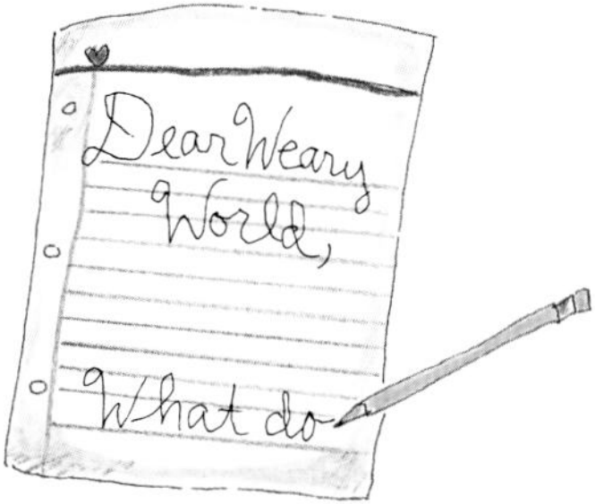
Dear Weary
World,
What do

When our poor
hearts are
broken
in two

and we struggle
through lives that
no longer feel
        like our own?

We could gather together
a million clocks
so we'd have
time enough
to grieve.

We could hire birds
to sing outside our
windowsills

or find some huge umbrellas
to shelter us from
  weeping skies
  that cry
    in sympathy.

Could we lessen
our feelings of
    weariness

  by looking at life
    from a
  higher
      perspective,

from a place where
we'd know things
like
strolling

and riding a bike
were dear little
blessings we once
overlooked?

What if we promised,
each to the other,

We promise...

not to take anything
for granted again?

Like hot showers
and

fresh towels,

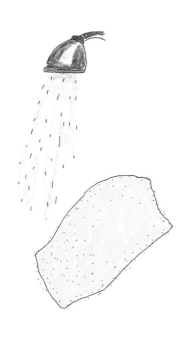

letters from
home
with a
photo
inside,

hot cups of
Coffee
and biscuits
with
jam.

or the sight
of
a flag
in
the
breeze

Dear Weary World,

what do we do
when our hearts
be gin
aching
for some way
to let in the sunshine
again?

Hello again!

We can hold hands
with each
other,

share kind words
that
heal,

The First Annual
" Too Seldom Said Day "
for the things we don't say enough

I
appreciate
you.

and realize

the strength
that we
all
possess.

We can go
   out to dinner
   and
   share in a
      laugh,

we can celebrate
birthdays,

sleep out under the
stars,

and go to
the
beach
and float on
the salty
blue waves

Dear Weary World,

Each day we'll
get better
one step at
a time,

and whether
it's sharing
        blue skies
    or sweaters

    or even
    just holding
        hands,

Together we'll
find it,
  the place
in our hearts
    where
        joy
      can begin

and where
we'll leave
feeling weary
behind.